KU-345-706

SQA

2016 SQA Past Papers With Answers

National 5
FRENCH

FREE
audio files to accompany this title can be accessed at
www.hoddergibson.co.uk
• Click on the turquoise 'Updates and Extras' box.
• Look for the 'SQA Papers Audio Files' heading and click the 'Browse' button beneath.
• You will then find the files listed by language and level.

2014, 2015 & 2016 Exams

Hodder Gibson Study Skills Advice – General	– page 3
Hodder Gibson Study Skills Advice – National 5 French	– page 5
2014 EXAM	– page 7
2015 EXAM	– page 37
2016 EXAM	– page 67
ANSWERS	– page 97

National 5 FRENCH

HODDER
GIBSON
AN HACHETTE UK COMPANY

This book contains the official SQA 2014, 2015 and 2016 Exams for National 5 French, with associated SQA-approved answers modified from the official marking instructions that accompany the paper.

In addition the book contains study skills advice. This advice has specially commissioned by Hodder Gibson, and has been written by experienced senior teachers and examiners in line with the new National 5 syllabus and assessment outlines. This is not SQA material but has been devised to provide further guidance for National 5 examinations.

Hodder Gibson is grateful to the copyright holders, as credited on the final page of the Answer Section, for permission to use their material. Every effort has been made to trace the copyright holders and to obtain their permission for the use of copyright material. Hodder Gibson will be happy to receive information allowing us to rectify any error or omission in future editions.

Hachette UK's policy is to use papers that are natural, renewable and recyclable products and made from wood grown in sustainable forests. The logging and manufacturing processes are expected to conform to the environmental regulations of the country of origin.

Orders: please contact Bookpoint Ltd, 130 Park Drive, Milton Park, Abingdon, Oxon OX14 4SE. Telephone: (44) 01235 827720. Fax: (44) 01235 400454. Lines are open 9.00–5.00, Monday to Saturday, with a 24-hour message answering service. Visit our website at www.hoddereducation.co.uk. Hodder Gibson can be contacted direct on: Tel: 0141 333 4650; Fax: 0141 404 8188; email: hoddergibson@hodder.co.uk

This collection first published in 2016 by
Hodder Gibson, an imprint of Hodder Education,
An Hachette UK Company
211 St Vincent Street
Glasgow G2 5QY

National 5 2014, 2015 and 2016 Exam Papers and Answers © Scottish Qualifications Authority. Study Skills section © Hodder Gibson. All rights reserved. Apart from any use permitted under UK copyright law, no part of this publication may be reproduced or transmitted in any form or by any means, electronic or mechanical, including photocopying and recording, or held within any information storage and retrieval system, without permission in writing from the publisher or under licence from the Copyright Licensing Agency Limited. Further details of such licences (for reprographic reproduction) may be obtained from the Copyright Licensing Agency Limited, Saffron House, 6–10 Kirby Street, London EC1N 8TS.

Typeset by Aptara, Inc.

Printed in the UK

A catalogue record for this title is available from the British Library

ISBN: 978-1-4718-9109-0

3 2 1

2017 2016

Introduction
Study Skills – what you need to know to pass exams!

Pause for thought

Many students might skip quickly through a page like this. After all, we all know how to revise. Do you really though?

Think about this:

"IF YOU ALWAYS DO WHAT YOU ALWAYS DO, YOU WILL ALWAYS GET WHAT YOU HAVE ALWAYS GOT."

Do you like the grades you get? Do you want to do better? If you get full marks in your assessment, then that's great! Change nothing! This section is just to help you get that little bit better than you already are.

There are two main parts to the advice on offer here. The first part highlights fairly obvious things but which are also very important. The second part makes suggestions about revision that you might not have thought about but which WILL help you.

Part 1

DOH! It's so obvious but …

Start revising in good time

Don't leave it until the last minute – this will make you panic.

Make a revision timetable that sets out work time AND play time.

Sleep and eat!

Obvious really, and very helpful. Avoid arguments or stressful things too – even games that wind you up. You need to be fit, awake and focused!

Know your place!

Make sure you know exactly **WHEN and WHERE** your exams are.

Know your enemy!

Make sure you know what to expect in the exam.

How is the paper structured?

How much time is there for each question?

What types of question are involved?

Which topics seem to come up time and time again?

Which topics are your strongest and which are your weakest?

Are all topics compulsory or are there choices?

Learn by DOING!

There is no substitute for past papers and practice papers – they are simply essential! Tackling this collection of papers and answers is exactly the right thing to be doing as your exams approach.

Part 2

People learn in different ways. Some like low light, some bright. Some like early morning, some like evening / night. Some prefer warm, some prefer cold. But everyone uses their BRAIN and the brain works when it is active. Passive learning – sitting gazing at notes – is the most INEFFICIENT way to learn anything. Below you will find tips and ideas for making your revision more effective and maybe even more enjoyable. What follows gets your brain active, and active learning works!

Activity 1 – Stop and review

Step 1

When you have done no more than 5 minutes of revision reading STOP!

Step 2

Write a heading in your own words which sums up the topic you have been revising.

Step 3

Write a summary of what you have revised in no more than two sentences. Don't fool yourself by saying, "I know it, but I cannot put it into words". That just means you don't know it well enough. If you cannot write your summary, revise that section again, knowing that you must write a summary at the end of it. Many of you will have notebooks full of blue/black ink writing. Many of the pages will not be especially attractive or memorable so try to liven them up a bit with colour as you are reviewing and rewriting. **This is a great memory aid, and memory is the most important thing.**

Activity 2 – Use technology!

Why should everything be written down? Have you thought about "mental" maps, diagrams, cartoons and colour to help you learn? And rather than write down notes, why not record your revision material?

What about having a text message revision session with friends? Keep in touch with them to find out how and what they are revising and share ideas and questions.

Why not make a video diary where you tell the camera what you are doing, what you think you have learned and what you still have to do? No one has to see or hear it, but the process of having to organise your thoughts in a formal way to explain something is a very important learning practice.

Be sure to make use of electronic files. You could begin to summarise your class notes. Your typing might be slow, but it will get faster and the typed notes will be easier to read than the scribbles in your class notes. Try to add different fonts and colours to make your work stand out. You can easily Google relevant pictures, cartoons and diagrams which you can copy and paste to make your work more attractive and **MEMORABLE**.

Activity 3 – This is it. Do this and you will know lots!

Step 1

In this task you must be very honest with yourself! Find the SQA syllabus for your subject (www.sqa.org.uk). Look at how it is broken down into main topics called MANDATORY knowledge. That means stuff you MUST know.

Step 2

BEFORE you do ANY revision on this topic, write a list of everything that you already know about the subject. It might be quite a long list but you only need to write it once. It shows you all the information that is already in your long-term memory so you know what parts you do not need to revise!

Step 3

Pick a chapter or section from your book or revision notes. Choose a fairly large section or a whole chapter to get the most out of this activity.

With a buddy, use Skype, Facetime, Twitter or any other communication you have, to play the game "If this is the answer, what is the question?". For example, if you are revising Geography and the answer you provide is "meander", your buddy would have to make up a question like "What is the word that describes a feature of a river where it flows slowly and bends often from side to side?".

Make up 10 "answers" based on the content of the chapter or section you are using. Give this to your buddy to solve while you solve theirs.

Step 4

Construct a wordsearch of at least 10 × 10 squares. You can make it as big as you like but keep it realistic. Work together with a group of friends. Many apps allow you to make wordsearch puzzles online. The words and phrases can go in any direction and phrases can be split. Your puzzle must only contain facts linked to the topic you are revising. Your task is to find 10 bits of information to hide in your puzzle, but you must not repeat information that you used in Step 3. DO NOT show where the words are. Fill up empty squares with random letters. Remember to keep a note of where your answers are hidden but do not show your friends. When you have a complete puzzle, exchange it with a friend to solve each other's puzzle.

Step 5

Now make up 10 questions (not "answers" this time) based on the same chapter used in the previous two tasks. Again, you must find NEW information that you have not yet used. Now it's getting hard to find that new information! Again, give your questions to a friend to answer.

Step 6

As you have been doing the puzzles, your brain has been actively searching for new information. Now write a NEW LIST that contains only the new information you have discovered when doing the puzzles. Your new list is the one to look at repeatedly for short bursts over the next few days. Try to remember more and more of it without looking at it. After a few days, you should be able to add words from your second list to your first list as you increase the information in your long-term memory.

FINALLY! Be inspired...

Make a list of different revision ideas and beside each one write **THINGS I HAVE** tried, **THINGS I WILL** try and **THINGS I MIGHT** try. Don't be scared of trying something new.

And remember – "FAIL TO PREPARE AND PREPARE TO FAIL!"

National 5 French

The course

The National 5 French course aims to enable you to develop the ability to read, listen, talk and write in French, that is to understand and use French, and to apply your knowledge and understanding of the language. The course offers the opportunity to develop detailed language skills in the real-life contexts of society, learning, employability and culture.

How the course is graded

The Course assessment will take the form of a performance and a written exam.

The performance will be a presentation and discussion with your teacher, which will be recorded and marked by your teacher.

This book will help you practise for the written exam you will sit in May.

The exams

Reading and Writing

- exam time: 1 hour 30 minutes
- total marks: 50
- weighting in final grade: 50%

What you have to do

- Read three passages of just under 200 words each, and answer questions about them in English.
- write 120–150 words in French in the form of an email, applying for a job or work placement: there will be six bullet points for you to address.

Listening

- exam time: 25 minutes
- total marks: 20
- weighting in final grade: 20%

What you have to do

- part 1: listen to a monologue in French, and answer questions in English
- part 2: listen to a dialogue In French, and answer questions about it in English.

How to improve your mark!

Every year, examiners notice the same kind of mistakes being made, and also they regularly come across some excellent work. They give advice in the three key areas of reading, listening and writing to help students do better. Here are some key points from their advice.

Reading

Make sure that your answers include detail in Reading. Pick out detail from longer chunks of language, rather than focusing on individual words. Read the whole message, then pick out the key points, using the questions as a guide as to where to look. Detailed answers are generally required, so pay particular attention to words like assez, très, trop, vraiment and to negatives. Make sure you get the details of numbers, day, times etc right.

Take care when using dictionaries where a word has more than one meaning. Learn to choose the correct meaning from a list of meanings in a dictionary.

Beware of faux amis: journée means day, not journey, travailler means work, not travel, for instance!

In responding to the questions in the Reading papers, you should be guided by the number of points awarded for each question. You should give as much detail in your answer as you have understood but should not put down everything which is in the original text, as you are wasting time. The question itself usually indicates the amount of information required by stating in bold, e.g. "Mention two of them". Often there are more than two possibilities, but choose the two you are happiest with and stick to them. Don't try to give alternatives, just choose the correct number. Note that there will be a question in one of the reading papers which asks about the overall purpose of the writing. This will always be a "supported" question, such as a box to tick or a true/false choice.

You should re-read your answers to make sure that they make sense and that your English expression is as good as it can be.

Listening

This is the paper that improves most with practice. So use the listening papers in this book several times, to get used to the format of the exam.

Not giving enough detail is still a major reason for candidates losing marks. Many answers are correct as far as they go but were not sufficiently detailed to score marks. The same rules as for Reading apply.

You hear each of the Listening texts three times, so make use of the third listening to check the accuracy and specific details of your answers.

Be sure you are able to give accurate answers through confident knowledge of numbers, common adjectives, weather expressions, prepositions and question words, so that some of the "easier" points of information are not lost through lack of sufficiently accurate details.

In responding to the questions in the Listening papers, you should be guided by the number of points awarded for each question, and by the wording of the question. You should give as much detail in your answer as you have understood but should not write down everything you hear. The question itself usually indicates the amount of information required by stating in bold, e.g. "Mention 2 of them".

Make sure you put a line through any notes you have made.

Writing

This, along with Talking, is where students do best. However, frequently, the language used by candidates tackling Writing dips to a basic level and leads to pieces not being truly developed. Make sure you have some good material prepared and learned, ready to use in the exam.

Also, where learners write pieces that are too lengthy, this certainly does not help their performance. So stick to the 20–30 words per bullet point.

The examiners say many of the pieces are vibrant and refreshing in terms of style and content. At the upper level, the majority of candidates write well, and the range of language used is impressive. So look at the success criteria in the answer section and try to model your Writing on it. This applies particularly to the last two bullet points.

You should ensure that you are careful when you read the information regarding the job you are applying for, and make sure your answer is tailored to fit that. Depending on the job, you may have to alter your strengths or the experience you are claiming.

You should refrain from writing long lists of things such as school subjects (and then repeating the list with a past or future verb tense) as part of your answers.

Use the dictionary to check the accuracy of what you have written (spelling, accents, genders etc.) but not to create new sentences, particularly when dealing with the last two bullet points. You should have everything you need prepared when you come into the exam.

Be aware of the extended criteria to be used in assessing performances in Writing, so that you know what is required in terms of content, accuracy and range and variety of language to achieve the good and very good categories. Ensure that your handwriting is legible (particularly when writing in French) and distinguish clearly between rough notes and what you wish to be considered as final answers. Make sure you score out your notes!

You should bear the following points in mind:

- there are six bullet points to answer: the first four are always the same, the last two vary from year to year
- each of the first four bullet points should have between 20 and 30 words to address it properly
- to get a mark of satisfactory or above, you must address the last two bullet points properly
- you should aim to have at least 15 words for each of these last two points, but do not try to write too much for these
- you will be assessed on how well you have answered the points, and on the accuracy of your language
- for a mark of good or very good, you should have some complex language, such as longer, varied sentences and conjunctions

Good luck!

Remember that the rewards for passing National 5 French are well worth it! Your pass will help you get the future you want for yourself. In the exam, be confident in your own ability. If you're not sure how to answer a question, trust your instincts and just give it a go anyway – keep calm and don't panic! GOOD LUCK!

NATIONAL 5

2014

N5

National
Qualifications
2014

Mark

X730/75/01

**French
Reading**

WEDNESDAY, 14 MAY

9:00 AM – 10:30 AM

Fill in these boxes and read what is printed below.

Full name of centre

Town

Forename(s)

Surname

Number of seat

Date of birth

Day   Month   Year

Scottish candidate number

Total marks — 30

Attempt ALL questions.

Write your answers clearly, in **English**, in the spaces provided in this booklet.

You may use a French dictionary.

Additional space for answers is provided at the end of this booklet. If you use this space you must clearly identify the question number you are attempting.

Use **blue** or **black** ink.

There is a separate question and answer booklet for Writing. You must complete your answer for Writing in the question and answer booklet for Writing.

Before leaving the examination room you must give both booklets to the Invigilator; if you do not, you may lose all the marks for this paper.

MARKS | DO NOT WRITE IN THIS MARGIN

Total marks — 30

Attempt ALL questions

Text 1

You are surfing the Internet and read this French article about a survey.

Est-ce que les jeunes Français reçoivent moins d'argent de poche qu'il y a cinq ans?

On a parlé avec 500 parents et leurs enfants. Voici les résultats !

Malgré la crise économique les parents continuent à donner de l'argent à leurs enfants. En fait, les jeunes reçoivent dix euros de plus par mois comparé à 2009. D'ailleurs, les parents disent que le montant augmente avec l'âge de l'enfant.

Que font-ils avec cet argent?

Chez les garçons il s'agit souvent des sorties en ville ou d'aller voir leur équipe préférée tandis que les filles ont plus tendance à économiser leur argent.

Pourquoi les parents donnent de l'argent?

Il y a des parents qui donnent de l'argent comme récompense, par exemple pour un bon bulletin scolaire ou pour les tâches ménagères faites à la maison. Ils offrent aussi de l'argent pour les anniversaires.

Finalement, la plupart des parents sont «pour» l'argent de poche car ça aide leurs enfants à gérer leur budget. S'ils le gèrent lorsqu'ils sont jeunes, ce sera plus facile quand ils seront adultes.

Questions

    (a) What is the first question of the survey?   1

_____

_____

MARKS | DO NOT WRITE IN THIS MARGIN

Text 1 Questions (continued)

(b) What was the result of the survey? Tick (✓) the correct statement.   **1**

Parents have stopped giving money.	
Parents give the same amount of money.	
The amount has increased by 10 Euros over the last 5 years.	

(c) Young people do different things with their money.

   (i) According to the survey, what do boys spend their money on? State **two** things.   **2**

   _____

   _____

   (ii) What do girls do with their money?   **1**

   _____

   _____

(d) Parents give money to their children at other times. When? State any **three** things.   **3**

   _____

   _____

   _____

(e) Most parents are in favour of pocket money. Why? State **two** things.   **2**

   _____

   _____

[Turn over

MARKS

Text 2

You read an article about learning languages.

Les langues ont une très grande importance. Apprendre une langue nous aide à apprécier le mode de vie d'autres pays et l'apprentissage d'une langue aide à mieux connaître sa propre langue.

C'est aussi un grand atout pour sa carrière professionnelle. Beaucoup d'employeurs veulent que leurs employés parlent au moins une langue étrangère.

Julien parle de son expérience.

«Quand j'étais à l'école les langues étrangères ne m'intéressaient pas car j'avais beaucoup de mal à m'exprimer.

Mais heureusement tout ça a bien changé. Après mes études à la fac, j'ai décidé d'apprendre l'anglais. Je n'arrivais pas à trouver du travail dans mon pays et donc on m'a conseillé d'apprendre une deuxième langue pour élargir mes possibilités d'emploi.

Bien sûr j'ai suivi des cours d'anglais mais j'ai aussi commencé à regarder les actualités télévisées en anglais et j'ai même changé le langage sur mon portable. Après quelques mois j'ai trouvé un travail en Angleterre. Depuis les langues sont devenues ma passion.

J'ai quelques conseils pour ceux qui veulent apprendre une langue. Il faut essayer de passer au moins un an dans le pays et de parler dès le début avec les habitants. Et surtout il ne faut pas avoir honte de faire des fautes, c'est tout à fait normal.»

Questions

(a) What do languages help you to do? State any **one** thing.

1

_____

_____

(b) Languages are also an asset in your professional career. Why? Tick (✓) the correct statement.

1

Many employers want their employees to speak at least one language.	
Employers want their employees to work abroad.	
You can get a better job.	

MARKS

Text 2 Questions (continued)

(c) Why was Julien not interested in languages when he was at school? State **one** thing.

1

_____

_____

(d) Why did he decide to learn English? State **two** things.

2

_____

_____

_____

(e) Apart from taking English lessons what else did he do to help improve his level of English? State **two** things.

2

_____

_____

(f) What advice does he have for those who want to learn languages? State any **two** things.

2

_____

_____

(g) What is Julien's overall opinion of learning languages? Tick (✓) the correct statement.

1

Languages should not be taught in school.	
You should only learn a language to get a good job.	
Languages are important in all aspects of life.	

[Turn over

MARKS

Text 3

Whilst in France you read an article about "la Fête des lumières" – the festival of lights.

La Fête des lumières de Lyon qui a lieu le 8 décembre est une des manifestations les plus célèbres de la période de Noël en France.

Les origines datent de 1850 quand il y a eu un concours pour créer une nouvelle statue pour la ville.

Pour fêter la nouvelle statue, tous les gens de Lyon ont allumé des bougies à leurs fenêtres, puis ils sont descendus dans la rue pour regarder la ville toute éclairée et partager ce moment avec leurs amis.

Maintenant cette fête attire plus de 4 millions de visiteurs. Ils viennent pour voir les jardins de fleurs illuminés, les feux d'artifices dans la vieille ville et les images projetées sur tous les bâtiments.

Si vous voulez participer à cette fête merveilleuse, il est conseillé de bien réserver une chambre d'hôtel à l'avance et de s'habiller chaudement car il peut faire très froid à Lyon.

Par contre les résidents du centre-ville ne sont pas tous contents du nombre de visiteurs qui viennent pour la fête. Ils se plaignent qu'il n'y a pas de place pour se garer, qu'il est impossible de dormir à cause du bruit et que les gens jettent leurs papiers par terre.

Questions

(a) What is the festival of lights? Complete the sentence.   1

The festival of lights is one of the most _____

events of the Christmas period in France.

(b) The first festival in 1850 was about a new statue. How did everyone in Lyon celebrate? State any **two** things.   2

_____

_____

MARKS | DO NOT WRITE IN THIS MARGIN

Text 3 Questions (continued)

(c) This festival today attracts more than 4 million visitors. What do they come to see? State **three** things.

3

_____

_____

_____

(d) What advice is there for people going to the festival? State **two** things.

2

_____

_____

(e) Why are some residents not happy about the number of visitors who come to the festival? State any **two** things.

2

_____

_____

[END OF QUESTION PAPER]

MARKS | DO NOT WRITE IN THIS MARGIN

ADDITIONAL SPACE FOR ANSWERS

MARKS

ADDITIONAL SPACE FOR ANSWERS

Page ten

[BLANK PAGE]

DO NOT WRITE ON THIS PAGE

N5

National Qualifications 2014

Mark

X730/75/02

French Writing

WEDNESDAY, 14 MAY

9:00 AM – 10:30 AM

Fill in these boxes and read what is printed below.

Full name of centre

Town

Forename(s)

Surname

Number of seat

Date of birth

Day   Month   Year

Scottish candidate number

Total marks — 20

Write your answer clearly, in **French**, in the space provided in this booklet.

You may use a French dictionary.

Additional space for answers is provided at the end of this booklet.

Use **blue** or **black** ink.

There is a separate question and answer booklet for Reading. You must complete your answers for Reading in the question and answer booklet for Reading.

Before leaving the examination room you must give both booklets to the Invigilator; if you do not, you may lose all the marks for this paper.

MARKS

Total marks — 20

You are preparing an application for the job advertised below and you write an e-mail in **French** to the company.

Employeur: La Belle Bourgogne, Visites Guidées

Titre du Poste: Assistant(e) touristique

Nous nécessitons du personnel d'été pour:

- préparer les pique-niques
- accueillir les touristes avant les visites
- nettoyer et ranger les camionnettes et le bureau à la fin de la journée

Essentiels:

- Une connaissance de la langue française
- Une bonne présentation

Renseignements: Pour plus de détails, contactez M Alligant:

e-mail: visites.bellebourgogne@orange.fr
adresse: 25 rue de Constantine
40260 Saulieu
Tél: 08 76 85 44 25
Fax: 08 76 85 44 26

To help you to write your e-mail, you have been given the following checklist.

You must include all of these points:

- Personal details (name, age, where you live)
- School/college/education experience until now
- Skills/interests you have which make you right for the job
- Related work experience
- Any link you may have with a French speaking country
- A request for information about the working hours.

Use all of the above to help you write the e-mail in **French**. The e-mail should be approximately 120–150 words. You may use a French dictionary.

MARKS

ANSWER SPACE

[Turn over

MARKS | DO NOT WRITE IN THIS MARGIN

ANSWER SPACE (continued)

MARKS | DO NOT WRITE IN THIS MARGIN

ANSWER SPACE (continued)

[Turn over

MARKS | DO NOT WRITE IN THIS MARGIN

ANSWER SPACE (continued)

[END OF QUESTION PAPER]

MARKS | DO NOT WRITE IN THIS MARGIN

ADDITIONAL SPACE FOR ANSWERS

MARKS | DO NOT WRITE IN THIS MARGIN

ADDITIONAL SPACE FOR ANSWERS

N5

National
Qualifications
2014

Mark

X730/75/03

French Listening

WEDNESDAY, 14 MAY

10:50 AM – 11:15 AM (approx)

Fill in these boxes and read what is printed below.

Full name of centre

Town

Forename(s)

Surname

Number of seat

Date of birth

Day	Month	Year
D D	M M	Y Y

Scottish candidate number

Total marks — 20

Attempt ALL questions.

Write your answers clearly, in **English**, in the spaces provided in this booklet. Additional space for answers is provided at the end of this booklet. If you use this space you must clearly identify the question number you are attempting.

Use **blue** or **black** ink.

You will hear two items in French. **Before you hear each item, you will have one minute to study the questions.** You will hear each item three times, with an interval of one minute between playings. You will then have time to answer the questions before hearing the next item.

You may take notes as you are listening to the French, but only in this booklet.

You may NOT use a French dictionary.

You are not allowed to leave the examination room until the end of the test.

Before leaving the examination room you must give this booklet to the Invigilator; if you do not, you may lose all the marks for this paper.

MARKS | DO NOT WRITE IN THIS MARGIN

Total marks — 20

Attempt ALL questions

Item 1

Patricia talks about her part-time job.

(a) Why does Patricia love her job? State any **two** things.　　2

_____

_____

(b) She has to cycle to work. Why is this? State any **one** thing.　　1

_____

(c) She talks about what she has to do in the restaurant.

　　(i) What is her main job?　　1

　　_____

　　(ii) When there are a lot of customers, what else does she have to do? State any **one** thing.　　1

　　_____

(d) In her opinion what advantages does this job have? State any **two** things.　　2

_____

_____

(e) What is Patricia's overall opinion of her part-time job?

Tick (✓) the correct statement.　　1

She loves it, but she is badly paid.	
She loves it, but would rather meet her friends.	
She loves it, but it can be busy and tiring.	

MARKS | DO NOT WRITE IN THIS MARGIN

Item 2

You then listen to Philippe who asks Sylvie questions about her part-time job.

(a) How often does Sylvie work in the supermarket? Complete the sentence.   **1**

She works there _____ a week.

(b) Why does Sylvie get on well with her colleagues? State any **two** things.   **2**

_____

_____

(c) Sylvie's job has had an impact on her social life.

(i) What annoyed her when she started this job?   **1**

_____

_____

(ii) Why is the situation better for her now? State **two** things.   **2**

_____

_____

(d) How does she still manage to fit in her homework? State any **two** things.   **2**

_____

_____

(e) How will this experience of working help her find a job in the future? State any **two** things.   **2**

_____

_____

_____

(f) What are her plans for next year? State any **two** things.   **2**

_____

_____

[END OF QUESTION PAPER]

MARKS | DO NOT WRITE IN THIS MARGIN

ADDITIONAL SPACE FOR ANSWERS

MARKS | DO NOT WRITE IN THIS MARGIN

ADDITIONAL SPACE FOR ANSWERS

[BLANK PAGE]

DO NOT WRITE ON THIS PAGE

National Qualifications 2014

X730/75/13

French
Listening Transcript

WEDNESDAY, 14 MAY
10:50 AM – 11:15 AM (approx)

This paper must not be seen by any candidate.

The material overleaf is provided for use in an emergency only (eg the recording or equipment proving faulty) or where permission has been given in advance by SQA for the material to be read to candidates with additional support needs. The material must be read exactly as printed.

Instructions to reader(s)

For each item, read the English **once**, then read the French **three times**, with an interval of 1 minute between the three readings. On completion of the third reading, pause for the length of time indicated in brackets after the item, to allow the candidates to write their answers.

Where special arrangements have been agreed in advance to allow the reading of the material, those sections marked **(f)** should be read by a female speaker and those marked **(m)** by a male; those sections marked **(t)** should be read by the teacher.

(t)   **Item Number One**

Patricia talks about her part-time job.

You now have one minute to study the questions for Item Number One.

(f)   Moi, je travaille les week-ends dans un restaurant au centre-ville. J'adore mon petit boulot car il y a une bonne ambiance au restaurant, les mêmes clients reviennent régulièrement, et le travail n'est jamais ennuyeux.

Je commence à neuf heures et je termine à trois heures. Je dois aller au travail à vélo, même quand il pleut, parce que j'habite un village assez loin du restaurant et il n'y a pas de transports en commun.

En ce qui concerne mes tâches, mon rôle principal est de servir les boissons. Mais, quand il y a beaucoup de clients je dois aider dans la cuisine et débarrasser les tables. Ces journées sont très chargées et je suis souvent très fatiguée!

A mon avis les avantages de ce travail sont que les clients sont généreux et nous laissent de bons pourboires et en plus, je peux manger gratuitement au restaurant les jours de travail.

Ce travail me plaît tellement qu'un jour j'aimerais avoir mon propre restaurant.

(*2 minutes*)

(t) Item Number Two

You then listen to Philippe who asks Sylvie questions about her part-time job.

You now have one minute to study the questions for Item Number Two.

(m) Bonjour Sylvie, ça va ?

(f) Oui, bien merci.

(m) Comment va ton nouveau boulot au supermarché?

(f) Bien, c'est assez intéressant et en plus ça me change du travail scolaire. J'y travaille deux soirs par semaine, ce qui me convient.

(m) Comment est-ce que tu t'entends avec tes collègues?

(f) Je m'entends bien avec eux. C'est super car il y en a beaucoup qui ont le même âge que moi, donc on a des choses en commun et on aime sortir ensemble.

(m) Est-ce que ton travail a changé ta vie sociale?

(f) Oui certainement. Au début ça m'embêtait que mes amis du lycée se retrouvent au café sans moi. Mais tout va mieux maintenant parce qu'on sort tous les vendredis soirs et on fait la fête ensemble.

(m) Est- ce que tu as assez de temps pour faire tes devoirs?

(f) Oui bien sûr, mais il faut que je m'organise. Par exemple, je consacre les dimanches à faire mes devoirs et en plus je ne passe pas des heures devant la télévision comme avant.

(m) Tu crois que ce travail va t'aider à l'avenir?

(f) Oui, je crois que cette expérience va beaucoup m'aider quand je chercherai un travail plus tard. D'abord j'ai appris comment gérer mon temps. Et puis, j'ai plus de confiance pour parler aux gens que je ne connais pas et je dirais que je suis devenue plus responsable.

(m) Et quels sont tes projets pour l'année prochaine?

(f) Je n'en suis pas encore sûre. Soit je chercherai un emploi à plein-temps soit je passerai un an à voyager en Europe.

(m) Très bien, tu travailles ce soir ?

(f) Oui, d'ailleurs il faut que je me dépêche, à bientôt.

(2 minutes)

(t) End of test.

Now look over your answers.

[END OF TRANSCRIPT]

[BLANK PAGE]

DO NOT WRITE ON THIS PAGE

NATIONAL 5

2015

FOR OFFICIAL USE

N5

National Qualifications 2015

Mark

X730/75/01

French Reading

FRIDAY, 22 MAY

9:00 AM – 10:30 AM

Fill in these boxes and read what is printed below.

Full name of centre

Town

Forename(s)

Surname

Number of seat

Date of birth

Day Month Year

Scottish candidate number

Total marks — 30

Attempt ALL questions.

Write your answers clearly, in **English**, in the spaces provided in this booklet.

You may use a French dictionary.

Additional space for answers is provided at the end of this booklet. If you use this space you must clearly identify the question number you are attempting.

Use **blue** or **black** ink.

There is a separate question and answer booklet for Writing. You must complete your answer for Writing in the question and answer booklet for Writing.

Before leaving the examination room you must give both booklets to the Invigilator; if you do not, you may lose all the marks for this paper.

MARKS | DO NOT WRITE IN THIS MARGIN

Total marks — 30

Attempt ALL questions

Text 1

Your friend shows you an article in a French newspaper.

Les petits boulots : mode d'emploi

Lola est une collégienne de quinze ans. Elle voudrait travailler pour payer ses vêtements et pour mettre de l'argent de côté pour un voyage. Cependant ce n'est pas très facile pour les jeunes de trouver du travail.

«*Personne ne veut me donner du travail! J'ai demandé à une copine de ma mère qui tient un magasin et j'ai même appelé le patron d'une grande entreprise! On m'a dit que j'étais trop jeune et ils m'ont conseillé d'attendre deux ou trois ans. Ce n'est pas juste!!*»

Lola n'est pas la seule. La loi en France est très stricte. Les jeunes de moins de seize ans ne peuvent travailler que pendant les vacances scolaires et seulement si ces vacances durent quinze jours ou plus. On ne peut pas travailler plus de cinq heures par jour.

Alors, que doit-on faire pour gagner un peu d'argent?

Et bien, il faut profiter de la famille et des voisins! Aider des personnes âgées à faire des tâches ménagères, donner des cours particuliers à des élèves plus jeunes ou encore tondre le gazon. Mais attention – pour pratiquer tous ces petits boulots, il vous faudra une autorisation parentale. Comme la vie est dure!

Questions

(a) Lola would like to find a job. Why? Complete the sentence.   2

She would like to find a job to pay for her _____

and put some money away for _____.

(b) Lola talks about her job search. What did she do to find a job? State **two** things.   2

_____

_____

MARKS

Text 1 Questions (continued)

(c) Employers told her she was too young. What advice did they give her?   1

_____

(d) The law in France is very strict for workers under the age of sixteen. What are the rules? State any **two** things.   2

_____

_____

(e) The article suggests you can do some work for your family or neighbours. What could you do? State **three** things.   3

_____

_____

_____

[Turn over

MARKS | DO NOT WRITE IN THIS MARGIN

Text 2

You read an article which talks about the use of the Internet to support learning.

Internet et les études

L'usage d'Internet est devenu de plus en plus répandu à travers la France et on dit que c'est un outil de travail indispensable de nos jours. Les avantages sont nombreux — les étudiants peuvent faire des recherches et communiquer avec les gens partout dans le monde, tout en apprenant l'informatique.

La plupart des parents parlent aussi des bénéfices de l'Internet pour aider leurs enfants avec leurs devoirs. Par exemple, l'enfant peut essayer de trouver de l'aide par lui-même ou ses parents peuvent se renseigner pour informer l'enfant.

Néanmoins, il y a aussi des aspects négatifs: en passant des heures devant un écran on perd le contact avec la réalité et on lit moins de livres. Certaines personnes sortent de moins en moins car ils préfèrent rester chez eux à discuter avec leurs amis virtuels. Et attention! Il ne faut pas toujours croire à tout ce qu'on lit sur Internet.

Quant aux professeurs . . . oui, ils voient les avantages apportés par l'internet mais plusieurs problèmes se présentent. Par exemple, il n'y a pas assez d'ordinateurs dans les salles de classe, le système d'informatique est souvent en panne et il est parfois difficile d'accéder aux sites intéressants à l'école.

Questions

(a) The Internet has become more and more widespread in France. Which statement supports this? Tick (✓) the correct box.   **1**

People work more at home on the Internet.	
The Internet is an essential tool at work.	
You can book your travel in advance using the Internet.	

(b) What are the advantages of the Internet for students? State any **two** things.   **2**

_____

_____

MARKS | DO NOT WRITE IN THIS MARGIN

Text 2 Questions (continued)

(c) Young people often use the Internet to help with their homework. What benefits do parents see in this? State any **one** thing.

1

_____

(d) There are some negative aspects of using the Internet.

    (i) What could happen if you spend hours on the computer? State any **one** thing.

1

    _____

    (ii) People are going out less. Why?

1

    _____

    _____

    (iii) What do you need to be careful of when you are on the Internet?

1

    _____

    _____

(e) Teachers highlight a number of problems. What are they? State any **two** things.

2

_____

_____

(f) What is the author's overall opinion about the Internet to support learning? Tick (✓) the correct box.

1

The Internet should be forbidden in schools.	
All learning should be done using the Internet.	
The Internet can support learning when and where appropriate.	

[Turn over

Text 3

You read an article about food waste.

C'est quoi, le gaspillage alimentaire*?

Le gaspillage alimentaire commence dès la production. Les supermarchés veulent vendre seulement de beaux produits, par exemple, des tomates bien rondes ou des pommes parfaites! Ceci oblige les producteurs de fruits et légumes à faire une sélection stricte et par conséquent, les fruits et légumes qui ont le moindre défaut finissent à la poubelle.

Le gaspillage vient aussi de nos habitudes de consommation. Bien souvent, nous achetons plus que ce que nous consommons réellement, et on jette environ 20% des aliments achetés.

Quelles sont les conséquences de ce gaspillage?

D'abord, l'argent utilisé pour produire ces aliments est gâché. Ensuite, il faut traiter tous ces déchets. Finalement, ce recyclage est une activité qui demande beaucoup d'énergie.

Que peut-on faire pour réduire le gaspillage?

Il existe des solutions très simples pour moins gaspiller à la maison: on devrait faire une liste des courses et n'acheter que la quantité de produits nécessaires. N'oubliez pas: on peut toujours congeler ce qui reste au frigo.

*Le gaspillage alimentaire — food waste

Questions

(a) Complete the following sentence. **1**

Supermarkets only want to sell beautiful produce such as really round

tomatoes and _____ .

(b) Supermarket policy affects fruit and vegetable producers.

   (i) What do the producers have to do? **1**

   _____

   (ii) What happens because of this? **1**

   _____

   _____

Text 3 Questions (continued)

MARKS

(c) In what ways do the habits of consumers contribute to the amount of food waste? State **two** things.

2

_____

_____

(d) Wasting food has consequences. State any **two** examples of this.

2

_____

_____

(e) What can each household do to help? State **three** things.

3

_____

_____

_____

[END OF QUESTION PAPER]

MARKS | DO NOT WRITE IN THIS MARGIN

ADDITIONAL SPACE FOR ANSWERS

MARKS DO NOT WRITE IN THIS MARGIN

ADDITIONAL SPACE FOR ANSWERS

[BLANK PAGE]

DO NOT WRITE ON THIS PAGE

N5

National
Qualifications
2015

Mark

X730/75/02

French
Writing

FRIDAY, 22 MAY

9:00 AM – 10:30 AM

Fill in these boxes and read what is printed below.

Full name of centre

Town

Forename(s)

Surname

Number of seat

Date of birth

Day	Month	Year

Scottish candidate number

Total marks — 20

Write your answer clearly, in **French**, in the space provided in this booklet.

You may use a French dictionary.

Additional space for answers is provided at the end of this booklet.

Use **blue** or **black** ink.

There is a separate question and answer booklet for Reading. You must complete your answers for Reading in the question and answer booklet for Reading.

Before leaving the examination room you must give both booklets to the Invigilator; if you do not, you may lose all the marks for this paper.

| DO NOT WRITE IN THIS MARGIN

Total marks — 20

You are preparing an application for the job advertised below and you write an e-mail in **French** to the company.

Colonie de Vacances
Pour les enfants 5 – 14 ans

Le travail en plein air vous attire?

Vous aimez travailler en équipe?

Vous êtes dynamique?

Vous aimez les enfants?

Le Jardin des Enfants en Normandie

Cherche

animateur/animatrice

Pour les mois de juin à septembre

On vous attend!

To help you to write your e-mail, you have been given the following checklist. You must include **all** of these points

- Personal details (name, age, where you live)
- School/college/education experience until now
- Skills/interests you have which make you right for the job
- Related work experience
- The reasons why you would like to work with children
- An enquiry about what there is to do in the area on your days off

Use all of the above to help you write the e-mail in **French**. The e-mail should be approximately 120–150 words. You may use a French dictionary.

MARKS DO NOT WRITE IN THIS MARGIN

ANSWER SPACE

[Turn over

_____

_____

_____

_____

_____

_____

_____

_____

_____

_____

_____

_____

_____

_____

_____

_____

_____

_____

_____

_____

_____

_____

_____

_____

_____

_____

MARKS | DO NOT WRITE IN THIS MARGIN

ANSWER SPACE (continued)

MARKS DO NOT WRITE IN THIS MARGIN

ANSWER SPACE (continued)

Page five **[Turn over**

MARKS | DO NOT WRITE IN THIS MARGIN

ANSWER SPACE (continued)

[END OF QUESTION PAPER]

MARKS | DO NOT WRITE IN THIS MARGIN

ADDITIONAL SPACE FOR ANSWERS

MARKS | DO NOT WRITE IN THIS MARGIN

ADDITIONAL SPACE FOR ANSWERS

N5

National Qualifications 2015

Mark ☐

X730/75/03

**French
Listening**

FRIDAY, 22 MAY

10:50 AM – 11:15 AM (approx)

Fill in these boxes and read what is printed below.

Full name of centre

Town

Forename(s)

Surname

Number of seat

Date of birth

Day   Month   Year

Scottish candidate number

Total marks — 20

Attempt ALL questions.

You will hear two items in French. **Before you hear each item, you will have one minute to study the questions.** You will hear each item three times, with an interval of one minute between playings. You will then have time to answer the questions before hearing the next item.

You may NOT use a French dictionary.

Write your answers clearly, in **English**, in the spaces provided in this booklet. Additional space for answers is provided at the end of this booklet. If you use this space you must clearly identify the question number you are attempting.

Use **blue** or **black** ink.

You are not allowed to leave the examination room until the end of the test.

Before leaving the examination room you must give this booklet to the Invigilator; if you do not, you may lose all the marks for this paper.

MARKS | DO NOT WRITE IN THIS MARGIN

Total marks — 20

Attempt ALL questions

Item 1

Whilst in France you listen to a young actor who is speaking on a local radio station.

(a) When did the film festival start?   1

_____

_____

(b) What will a 30 Euro ticket allow you to do? State any **one** thing.   1

_____

(c) You can see the films in their original language. What are the advantages of this? State **two** things.   2

_____

_____

(d) After some films you can take part in a debate. What will you have the chance to do there? State any **two** things.   2

_____

_____

(e) The actor talks about her film. What is it about? State any **one** thing.   1

_____

_____

(f) What is the purpose of the film festival? Tick (✓) the correct box.   1

To make money	
To promote international films	
To encourage young people to become actors	

Item 2

MARKS | DO NOT WRITE IN THIS MARGIN

Christophe talks to Julie about French cinema and television.

(a) Why is Julie really happy? State any **one** thing.

1

_____

(b) What does Julie love about going to the cinema? Tick (✓) the **two** correct boxes.

2

Eating popcorn and hotdogs	
Watching films on a big screen	
Sharing emotions with friends	
Enjoying the atmosphere	

(c) She says Danny Boon is her favourite French actor. What else does she say about him? State any **one** thing.

1

_____

(d) Why does she not like old French films? State any **two** things.

2

_____

_____

(e) Name any **two** advantages she gives of watching a film at home.

2

_____

_____

(f) What annoys her about French television? State any **two** things.

2

_____

_____

(g) Why does she like watching Channel 5? State **two** things.

2

_____

_____

[END OF QUESTION PAPER]

MARKS | DO NOT WRITE IN THIS MARGIN

ADDITIONAL SPACE FOR ANSWERS

MARKS | DO NOT WRITE IN THIS MARGIN

ADDITIONAL SPACE FOR ANSWERS

Page five

[BLANK PAGE]

DO NOT WRITE ON THIS PAGE

National Qualifications 2015

X730/75/13

French
Listening Transcript

FRIDAY, 22 MAY

10:50 AM – 11:15 AM (approx)

This paper must not be seen by any candidate.

The material overleaf is provided for use in an emergency only (eg the recording or equipment proving faulty) or where permission has been given in advance by SQA for the material to be read to candidates with additional support needs. The material must be read exactly as printed.

Instructions to reader(s)

For each item, read the English **once**, then read the French **three times**, with an interval of 1 minute between the three readings. On completion of the third reading, pause for the length of time indicated in brackets after the item, to allow the candidates to write their answers.

Where special arrangements have been agreed in advance to allow the reading of the material, those sections marked **(f)** should be read by a female speaker and those marked **(m)** by a male; those sections marked **(t)** should be read by the teacher.

(t) **Item Number One**

Whilst in France you listen to a young actor who is speaking on a local radio station.

You now have one minute to study the questions for Item Number One.

(f) Bonjour à tous. Je suis là aujourd'hui pour vous parler du festival international des films ainsi que de mon nouveau film.

Le festival a commencé il y a sept ans et chaque année il devient de plus en plus populaire.

Il dure une semaine et il y a beaucoup de films à voir. Vous pouvez acheter un billet pour 30 euros qui vous donne le droit d'aller voir 20 films de votre choix.

Les avantages d'assister au festival sont nombreux. Les films sont en version originale et donc vous pouvez faire la connaissance de différentes cultures et améliorer votre compréhension des langues étrangères.

Après quelques films il y aura la possibilité de participer à un débat. Vous aurez l'occasion de donner votre avis sur le film, rencontrer les acteurs et aussi de vous faire de nouveaux amis.

Cette année vous pourrez voir le film dans lequel j'ai joué. Mon film raconte l'histoire d'une française qui commence une nouvelle carrière en Espagne. Il est à la fois drôle mais aussi émouvant. Je ne vous en dis pas plus, venez le voir. A bientôt.

(2 minutes)

(t) Item Number Two

Christophe talks to Julie about French cinema and television.

You now have one minute to study the questions for Item Number Two.

(m) Bonjour Julie, comment ça va?

(f) Ça va super bien. C'est le début des vacances et en plus c'est mon anniversaire alors tout va bien.

(m) Génial! tu as des projets pour ce soir ?

(f) Oui, je vais aller au cinéma avec mes copains.

(m) Tu aimes le cinéma ?

(f) Oui, j'adore ça. J'y vais au moins une fois par semaine. Il n'y a rien de mieux que de regarder des films sur un grand écran et de partager ses émotions avec des amis.

(m) Quels genres de film préfères-tu ?

(f) Je n'ai pas de genre préféré mais mon acteur français préféré est Danny Boon. Il me fait vraiment rire et j'aime son accent du nord de la France.

(m) Y-a-t-il des films que tu n'aimes pas ?

(f) Je n'aime pas tellement les vieux films français. Ils sont toujours trop longs, le langage utilisé est très démodé et il y a très peu d'action.

(m) Aimes-tu regarder les films à la maison aussi ?

(f) Je préfère aller au cinéma mais il y a des avantages à regarder les films à la maison aussi. Si on n'aime pas le film on peut changer de chaîne, si on veut aller aux toilettes on peut le pauser et bien sûr c'est gratuit.

(m) Aimes-tu regarder la télé ?

(f) Ça dépend. Ce qui m'énerve à la télé française, c'est qu'il y a des publicités toutes les dix minutes, qu'il y a trop de feuilletons américains et que tous les matins il y a énormément de jeux stupides.

(m) Y-a-t-il quand même quelques bonnes émissions à la télé?

(f) Oui, j'aime regarder la 5. On peut y voir des documentaires très intéressants et ce que j'aime le plus, c'est qu'il y a souvent des émissions en allemand.

(m) Oh c'est bien ça, je devrais la regarder moi aussi. Ecoute, je te souhaite de bonnes vacances et bien sûr un joyeux anniversaire.

(2 minutes)

(t) End of test.

Now look over your answers.

[END OF TRANSCRIPT]

[BLANK PAGE]

DO NOT WRITE ON THIS PAGE

NATIONAL 5

2016

N5

National Qualifications 2016

Mark

X730/75/01

French Reading

MONDAY, 16 MAY

1:00 PM — 2:30 PM

Fill in these boxes and read what is printed below.

Full name of centre

Town

Forename(s)

Surname

Number of seat

Date of birth

Day　Month　Year

Scottish candidate number

Total marks — 30

Attempt ALL questions.

Write your answers clearly, in **English**, in the spaces provided in this booklet.

You may use a French dictionary.

Additional space for answers is provided at the end of this booklet. If you use this space you must clearly identify the question number you are attempting.

Use **blue** or **black** ink.

There is a separate question and answer booklet for Writing. You must complete your answer for Writing in the question and answer booklet for Writing.

Before leaving the examination room you must give both booklets to the Invigilator; if you do not, you may lose all the marks for this paper.

MARKS | DO NOT WRITE IN THIS MARGIN

Total marks — 30

Attempt ALL questions

Text 1

You read the following article about Paris Plage, a beach in the centre of Paris.

Chaque été depuis treize ans, un coin de Paris se transforme en plage de sable fin sur la rive droite de la Seine*.

C'est vraiment un lieu pour tout le monde: par exemple, les enfants peuvent participer aux concours des châteaux de sable ou faire voler des cerfs-volants et les adultes peuvent tout simplement se détendre au soleil en lisant un livre.

Il y a un écran géant en face de la plage pour ceux qui ne veulent pas rater les événements sportifs de l'été.

Olivier, 18 ans, est grand fan de la plage de la capitale. Il dit, «C'est génial pour les jeunes parisiens parce qu'il y en a beaucoup qui n'ont pas la possibilité d'aller au bord de la mer. Ils peuvent aller à cette plage sans quitter Paris. L'année dernière, j'y suis allé chaque après-midi pendant les grandes vacances. C'était un bon point de rencontre pour moi et mes amis et c'était gratuit!»

Farid n'est pas d'accord. «Paris Plage n'est pas une vraie plage car on n'a même pas le droit de se baigner. Je préférerais aller à une station balnéaire ou à une piscine en plein air.»

la Seine* – the name of the river in Paris

Questions

(a) Complete the sentence.   1

There has been a beach in Paris every summer for

_____.

(b) The beach has something for everyone.

(i) What is there for children? State **two** things.   2

_____

_____

MARKS | DO NOT WRITE IN THIS MARGIN

Text 1 Questions (continued)

(b) (continued)

(ii) What can adults do there? State any **one** thing.

1

_____

_____

(c) There is also a giant screen. Who can benefit from this?

1

_____

_____

(d) Olivier thinks that the beach is great for young Parisians. Why?

2

_____

_____

(e) Olivier went to the beach every afternoon last year. What does he say about it? State any **one** thing.

1

_____

_____

(f) Farid says Paris Plage is not a real beach.

(i) Why does he think this?

1

_____

_____

(ii) What would he prefer to do? State any **one** thing.

1

_____

[Turn over

MARKS | DO NOT WRITE IN THIS MARGIN

Text 2

You read an article about life in the city and in the countryside.

De nos jours il y a beaucoup de gens qui cherchent à vivre à la campagne. Ils veulent passer plus de temps à l'extérieur et se sentir plus en sécurité.

Mais est-ce que cette vie est vraiment meilleure que la vie en ville?

Voici un témoignage de Cécile qui a vécu les deux vies.

«Je viens d'un petit village mais je n'aimais pas y vivre. Il n'y avait rien à faire pour les jeunes, donc je m'ennuyais beaucoup.

Donc à l'âge de 17 ans je suis partie pour trouver du travail en ville. J'ai toute de suite adoré la vie en ville. J'aimais le fait que personne ne me connaissait et qu'il y avait un choix de divertissements. Mais après quelques années, j'ai changé d'avis. La circulation commençait à m'énerver et j'étais toujours pressée.

J'ai donc décidé d'acheter une maison secondaire à la campagne et je ne le regrette pas. J'ai deux chiens qui adorent courir dans les champs et je peux oublier tous les soucis de la vie quotidienne.

Personnellement je crois que ma situation est idéale car je mène une vie équilibrée. Je profite de l'animation de la ville et de la tranquillité de la campagne.»

Questions

(a) Why do many people want to live in the countryside? State **two** things. 2

_____

_____

(b) What does Cécile say about the small village where she lived? Tick (✓) the correct statement. 1

Everyone knew everyone.	
She was really bored.	
There were not many young people.	

MARKS | DO NOT WRITE IN THIS MARGIN

Text 2 Questions (continued)

(c) Cécile moved to the city when she was 17. What did she like about city life at first? State **two** things.

2

_____

_____

(d) In what ways did her opinion of city life change after a few years? State any **one** thing.

1

_____

_____

(e) She has no regrets about having bought a house in the country. Why? State **two** things.

2

_____

_____

(f) Why does she think she has a good balance in her life now? State **two** things.

2

_____

_____

[Turn over

MARKS | DO NOT WRITE IN THIS MARGIN

Text 3

You read an article where a student, Michel, talks about work experience.

Je suis étudiant à la faculté de droit et comme la plupart des étudiants j'ai fait un stage en entreprise chaque été. C'est un moyen d'avoir de l'expérience pratique et de gagner un peu d'argent.

Cependant, trouver un bon stage n'est pas toujours facile. On a une chance sur deux de tomber sur un stage "perte-de-temps". Dans certaines entreprises on a trop de responsabilités tandis que dans d'autres on sert le café, c'est tout. En même temps, quand on est stagiaire*, il est parfois difficile de gérer de nouvelles tâches.

Moi, j'ai fait deux stages bien différents. Le premier était épuisant et en plus, le patron était toujours de mauvaise humeur et j'avais peur de poser des questions si j'avais un problème. Par contre, le deuxième stage était une expérience positive. J'ai appris énormément de choses, j'ai assisté aux réunions importantes et on m'a donné des conseils régulièrement.

Enfin, ayant parlé avec d'autres stagiaires et après mes propres expériences, je peux affirmer que la qualité du stage dépend du responsable de la formation.

*stagiaire = person doing work experience

Questions

(a) How does Michel describe work experience? Complete the following sentence.   **2**

It is a way of _____

and _____ .

(b) Why it is not always easy to find a good work placement? State any **two** things.   **2**

_____

_____

(c) What do those doing work experience sometimes find difficult?   **1**

_____

_____

MARKS | DO NOT WRITE IN THIS MARGIN

Text 3 Questions (continued)

(d) Michel goes on to describe his two work placements.

   (i) As well as being exhausting, what does Michel say about his first placement? State **two** things.   **2**

_____

_____

   (ii) What made Michel's second placement a positive experience? State any **two** things.   **2**

_____

_____

(e) What is Michel's overall opinion of work experience? Tick (✓) the correct statement.   **1**

It is a waste of time and you are not paid any money.	
It is the only way of getting a job abroad.	
It can be a positive experience but it depends on the company.	

[END OF QUESTION PAPER]

MARKS

DO NOT WRITE IN THIS MARGIN

ADDITIONAL SPACE FOR ANSWERS

MARKS DO NOT WRITE IN THIS MARGIN

ADDITIONAL SPACE FOR ANSWERS

[BLANK PAGE]

DO NOT WRITE ON THIS PAGE

N5

National Qualifications 2016

Mark

X730/75/02

French Writing

MONDAY, 16 MAY
1:00 PM — 2:30 PM

Fill in these boxes and read what is printed below.

Full name of centre

Town

Forename(s)

Surname

Number of seat

Date of birth
Day   Month   Year   Scottish candidate number

Total marks — 20

Write your answer clearly, in **French**, in the space provided in this booklet.

You may use a French dictionary.

Additional space for answers is provided at the end of this booklet.

Use **blue** or **black** ink.

There is a separate question and answer booklet for Reading. You must complete your answers for Reading in the question and answer booklet for Reading.

Before leaving the examination room you must give both booklets to the Invigilator; if you do not, you may lose all the marks for this paper.

MARKS

Total marks — 20

You are preparing an application for the job advertised below and you write an e-mail in **French** to the company.

Employeur: Chocolaterie 'Les délices charentaises'

Titre du Poste: Vendeur/vendeuse

Profil: Accueillir et conseiller les clients, aider à la caisse, ranger la boutique, savoir parler l'anglais et le français.

Renseignements: Pour plus de détails, contactez

Mme Laurent au courriel: chocolaterie.delicescharentaises@gmail.com

Adresse: 38 rue du Château
18570 Graves Saint -Amant

Tél: 05 43 92 06 34
Fax: 05 43 92 06 35

To help you to write your e-mail, you have been given the following checklist.
You must include **all** of these points

- Personal details (name, age, where you live)
- School/college/education experience until now
- Skills/interests you have which make you right for the job
- Related work experience
- The dates you would be available to work there
- Ask a question about the job.

Use all of the above to help you write the e-mail in **French**. The e-mail should be approximately 120–150 words. You may use a French dictionary.

MARKS DO NOT WRITE IN THIS MARGIN

ANSWER SPACE

_____

_____

_____

_____

_____

_____

_____

_____

_____

_____

_____

_____

_____

_____

_____

_____

_____

_____

_____

_____

_____

_____

_____

_____

_____

_____

_____

_____

_____

_____

_____

MARKS | DO NOT WRITE IN THIS MARGIN

ANSWER SPACE (continued)

Page four

MARKS

ANSWER SPACE (continued)

MARKS | DO NOT WRITE IN THIS MARGIN

ANSWER SPACE (continued)

[END OF QUESTION PAPER]

MARKS | DO NOT WRITE IN THIS MARGIN

ADDITIONAL SPACE FOR ANSWERS

MARKS | DO NOT WRITE IN THIS MARGIN

ADDITIONAL SPACE FOR ANSWERS

FOR OFFICIAL USE

N5

National Qualifications 2016

Mark

X730/75/03

French Listening

MONDAY, 16 MAY

2:50 PM — 3:20 PM (approx)

Fill in these boxes and read what is printed below.

Full name of centre

Town

Forename(s)

Surname

Number of seat

Date of birth

Day	Month	Year	Scottish candidate number

Total marks — 20

Attempt ALL questions.

You will hear two items in French. **Before you hear each item, you will have one minute to study the questions.** You will hear each item three times, with an interval of one minute between playings. You will then have time to answer the questions before hearing the next item.

You may NOT use a French dictionary.

Write your answers clearly, in **English**, in the spaces provided in this booklet. Additional space for answers is provided at the end of this booklet. If you use this space you must clearly identify the question number you are attempting.

Use **blue** or **black** ink.

You are not allowed to leave the examination room until the end of the test.

Before leaving the examination room you must give this booklet to the Invigilator; if you do not, you may lose all the marks for this paper.

MARKS | DO NOT WRITE IN THIS MARGIN

Total marks — 20

Attempt ALL questions

Item 1

Jean, a French student, speaks about a school exchange.

(a) When does Jean's school come to Scotland? State any **one** thing.

1

_____

_____

(b) Which personal details do pupils have to give their teachers before signing up for the exchange? State any **two** things.

2

_____

_____

(c) The pupils go to the Scottish school every morning. What other activities do they do:

    (i) in the afternoon? State any **two** things.

2

_____

_____

    (ii) in the evening with their host family? State any **one** thing.

1

_____

_____

(d) What did Jean particularly love about Scotland? State any **one** thing.

1

_____

_____

(e) What is the **main** benefit of taking part in a school exchange? Tick (✓) the correct statement.

1

It is a good way to get to know another country well	
You spend time away from home	
You have the opportunity to go away with your friends	

MARKS | DO NOT WRITE IN THIS MARGIN

Item 2

Jacques talks to Monique about her recent school exchange experience in Scotland.

(a) Why is Monique tired? State **two** things.

2

_____

_____

(b) Monique talks about the differences in the Scottish school.

    (i) What does she say about the school facilities? State any **one** thing.

1

_____

_____

    (ii) Why does she think Scottish pupils are lucky? State any **two** things.

2

_____

_____

(c) Monique took part in lessons in Scotland.

    (i) What happened in the history class? State any **one** thing.

1

_____

_____

    (ii) Why did she really enjoy the Spanish class? State **two** things.

2

_____

_____

(d) What did she not like about the school? State any **two** things.

2

_____

_____

[Turn over

MARKS

Item 2 (continued)

(e) What does Monique say about school uniform? Tick (✓) the two correct statements.

2

It is smart	
It is not expensive	
The pupils feel proud when they wear it	
It is not popular with the pupils	

[END OF QUESTION PAPER]

MARKS | DO NOT WRITE IN THIS MARGIN

ADDITIONAL SPACE FOR ANSWERS

MARKS DO NOT WRITE IN THIS MARGIN

ADDITIONAL SPACE FOR ANSWERS

National Qualifications 2016

X730/75/13

French
Listening Transcript

MONDAY, 16 MAY

2:50 PM — 3:20 PM (approx)

This paper must not be seen by any candidate.

The material overleaf is provided for use in an emergency only (eg the recording or equipment proving faulty) or where permission has been given in advance by SQA for the material to be read to candidates with additional support needs. The material must be read exactly as printed.

Instructions to reader(s)

For each item, read the English **once**, then read the French **three times**, with an interval of 1 minute between the three readings. On completion of the third reading, pause for the length of time indicated in brackets after the item, to allow the candidates to write their answers.

Where special arrangements have been agreed in advance to allow the reading of the material, those sections marked **(f)** should be read by a female speaker and those marked **(m)** by a male; those sections marked **(t)** should be read by the teacher.

(t) Item Number One

Jean, a French student, speaks about a school exchange.

You now have one minute to study the questions for Item Number One.

(m) Bonjour, je m'appelle Jean. Je vais vous parler de l'échange scolaire dans mon école. Tous les ans, nous passons une semaine au printemps en Ecosse.

Avant le séjour, chaque élève donne quelques détails personnels aux professeurs. Par exemple, des informations sur ses passe-temps, ses animaux domestiques, et s'il y a des choses qu'on n'aime pas manger. Ensuite, les profs essaient de mettre ensemble les élèves écossais et les élèves français qui partagent les mêmes intérêts.

A l'étranger, on loge chez son correspondant. Les journées sont très chargées. On passe les matinées en cours au collège. L'après-midi on va au parc d'attractions, on achète des cadeaux pour des amis ou on fait un tour de la ville. Le soir on reste en famille où on a l'occasion de goûter des spécialités du pays et on discute des événements de la journée.

J'ai vraiment adoré mon séjour en Ecosse. Les gens étaient vraiment chaleureux et le paysage était impressionnant. J'espère y retourner très bientôt. Je recommanderais un échange à tout le monde.

(2 minutes)

(t)   **Item Number Two**

Jacques talks to Monique about her recent school exchange experience in Scotland.

You now have one minute to study the questions for Item Number Two.

(m)   Salut Monique, tu es bien rentrée de ton échange scolaire?

(f)   Ça va merci mais je suis toujours un peu fatiguée après le voyage de vingt-quatre heures en car. En plus, on était vraiment occupé en Ecosse tous les jours.

(m)   Est-ce que tu as remarqué des différences au collège écossais?

(f)   Ben, oui. Il y avait beaucoup de différences. Par exemple, le bâtiment était bien équipé avec un grand terrain de sport. De plus les élèves écossais ont de la chance! Ils finissent les cours avant 16 heures, ils ont moins de devoirs et ils peuvent participer aux activités après l'école.

(m)   Est-ce que tu as participé aux cours?

(f)   Oui tous les jours. Par exemple en histoire il y avait un débat animé et on a fait des sondages. La leçon que j'ai aimée le plus était l'espagnol car le prof était passionné par sa matière et expliquait bien ses cours.

(m)   Est ce qu'il y avait des choses que tu n'aimais pas?

(f)   Ce que j'ai trouvé moins bien était que la pause-déjeuner était trop courte; la plupart des élèves avait juste le temps de prendre un sandwich. De plus il n'y avait pas beaucoup de choix à la cantine et les repas n'étaient pas équilibrés.

(m)   Et que penses-tu de l'uniforme scolaire?

(f)   Tiens, ça fait un look très habillé. C'est une bonne idée de s'habiller différemment pour travailler au collège. A mon avis, les élèves sont fiers de porter leur uniforme et de faire partie d'une communauté.

(m)   Ça a l'air très intéressant; je vais peut-être y aller l'année prochaine.

(*2 minutes*)

(t)   **End of test.**

Now look over your answers.

[END OF TRANSCRIPT]

Page four

[BLANK PAGE]

DO NOT WRITE ON THIS PAGE

NATIONAL 5

Answers

NATIONAL 5 FRENCH 2014

Reading

1. (a) Do young (French) people/youths/children/ French people receive **less** (pocket) **money** than **5 years ago/2009**?

(b) The amount has increased by 10 Euros over the last 5 years.
(Third box ticked.)
(NB – More than one box ticked = 0 marks.)

(c) (i) • Going out **in town/city**/going **to town**/going to parties **in town**/outings **to the city**/evenings **in town**.
• (Going to) see/watch/support their **favourite/ preferred/best** team.
(NB – Going out to town to see their team = 1 mark.)

(ii) (Tend to) save their money.

(d) *Any three from:*
• To award their children/as a reward.
• For a **good** school report/doing **well at** school/**good** marks at school/**good** grades.
• For jobs done at home/helping at home/doing household tasks/chores/housework.
• For birthdays.

(e) • It helps children/young people to manage/they (learn to/can) manage their budget/money/ learn about money/can budget.
• It will be easier/easy when they are older/as adults/it helps them as adults/in the future

2. (a) *Any one from:*
• Appreciate (the way of life/lifestyle/form of life in) **another country/other countries**/the way people **in other countries** live/appreciate **other** ways of life.
• Helps us understand our (own) language (better).

(b) Many employers want their employees to speak at least one language.
(First box ticked.)
(NB – More than one box ticked = 0 marks.)

(c) • Found it **difficult/hard to/couldn't** express (himself/things)/**was bad at** expression/**wasn't good at/was bad at** expressing (himself/things)/ speaking/talking.
(NB – Tense irrelevant.)

(d) *Any two from:*
• Couldn't find a job **in his country/France** to find a job **in his country**/has never worked **in his country**.
• **Advised** to learn a language/Career Advisor told him to learn a language.
• To **widen/increase/enlarge/have more/other** job possibilities/help his chances of employment.
(NB – Easier to get a job in his own country = 1 mark.)

(e) • Watched **the news/current events/current affairs/ topical issues** (in English).
• Changed the language on his laptop/tablet/ computer/pc/mobile/phone/has the same language on his mobile/etc.

(f) *Any two from:*
• Spend (at least) **a year** in the country.
• (From the beginning) speak with the locals/ inhabitants/people who live there.
• Don't be afraid/embarrassed/ashamed to make **mistake(s)**/There is no shame in making **mistake(s)**/ There is nothing wrong with making **mistake(s)**/it is normal to make **mistake(s)**.

(g) Languages are important in all aspects of life.
(Third box ticked.)
(NB – More than one box ticked = 0 marks.)

3. (a) • Famous/Celebrated

(b) *Any two from:*
• Put/(lit/light/light up) candles **in the window**.
• **Went out/Went** (down) into the street(s).
• **Saw/Watched** the town illuminated/lit up.
• **Shared** this/the moment with (their) **friends/ enjoyed** with **friends/took part** with **friends**.
(NB – Tense irrelevant.)

(c) • Garden(s)/flowers **illuminated/lit up**/flower garden **light(s)**/garden of flowers **floodlit/floodlight** (accept different spellings of light).
• Fireworks **in the old town/city**.
• Pictures/images (projected) onto the building(s)/ the building(s) (all lit up) with images/Projections on building(s).

(d) • Book/reserve/(get a hotel/room) in **advance/ ahead/early**.
• Dress warmly/wear warm clothes/jacket/dress appropriately/wrap up warmly (it can be cold in Lyon).

(e) *Any two from:*
• Nowhere to **park**/hard **to park**/no **parking** places.
• Can't sleep because of the noise.
• (People) throwing/dropping paper/trash/rubbish/ litter(on the ground/earth/floor).
(NB – Litter (on its own) = 1 mark.)

Writing

Candidates will write a piece of extended writing in the modern language by addressing six bullet points. These bullet points will follow on from a job-related scenario. The bullet points will cover the four contexts of society, learning, employability and culture, to allow candidates to use and adapt learned material. The first four bullet points will be the same each year and the last two will change to suit the scenario. Candidates need to address these "unpredictable bullet points" in detail to access the full range of marks.

Category	Mark	Content	Accuracy	Language resource — variety, range, structures
Very good	20	The job advert has been addressed in a full and balanced way. The candidate uses detailed language. The candidate addresses the advert completely and competently, including **information in response to both unpredictable bullet points**. A range of verbs/verb forms, tenses and constructions is used. Overall this comes over as a competent, well-thought-out and serious application for the job.	The candidate handles all aspects of grammar and spelling accurately, although the language may contain one or two minor errors. Where the candidate attempts to use language more appropriate to Higher, a slightly higher number of inaccuracies need not detract from the overall very good impression.	The candidate is comfortable with the first person of the verb and generally uses a different verb in each sentence. Some modal verbs and infinitives may be used. There is good use of adjectives, adverbs and prepositional phrases and, where appropriate, word order. There may be a range of tenses. The candidate uses co-ordinating conjunctions and/or subordinate clauses where appropriate. The language of the e-mail flows well.
Good	16	The job advert has been addressed competently. There is less evidence of detailed language. The candidate uses a reasonable range of verbs/verb forms. Overall, the candidate has produced a genuine, reasonably accurate attempt at applying for the specific job, **even though he/she may not address one of the unpredictable bullet points.**	The candidate handles a range of verbs fairly accurately. There are some errors in spelling, adjective endings and, where relevant, case endings. Use of accents is less secure, where appropriate. Where the candidate is attempting to use more complex vocabulary and structures, these may be less successful, although basic structures are used accurately. There may be one or two examples of inaccurate dictionary use, especially in the unpredictable bullet points.	There may be repetition of verbs. There may be examples of listing, in particular when referring to school/college experience, without further amplification. There may be one or two examples of a co-ordinating conjunction, but most sentences are simple sentences. The candidate keeps to more basic vocabulary, particularly in response to either or both unpredictable bullet points.

Category	Mark	Content	Accuracy	Language resource — variety, range, structures
Satisfactory	12	The job advert has been addressed fairly competently. The candidate makes limited use of detailed language. The language is fairly repetitive and uses a limited range of verbs and fixed phrases, e.g. *I like, I go, I play*. The candidate copes fairly well with areas of personal details, education, skills, interests and work experience but does not deal fully with the two unpredictable bullet points **and indeed may not address either or both of the unpredictable bullet points.** On balance, however, the candidate has produced a satisfactory job application in the specific language.	The verbs are generally correct but may be repetitive. There are quite a few errors in other parts of speech — gender of nouns, cases, singular/plural confusion, for instance. Prepositions may be missing, e.g. *I go the town*. Overall, there is more correct than incorrect.	The candidate copes with the first and third person of a few verbs, where appropriate. A limited range of verbs is used. Sentences are basic and mainly brief. There is minimal use of adjectives, probably mainly after is e.g. *Chemistry is interesting*. The candidate has a weak knowledge of plurals. There may be several spelling errors, e.g. reversal of vowel combinations.
Unsatisfactory	8	The job advert has been addressed in an uneven manner and/or with insufficient use of detailed language. The language is repetitive, e.g. *I like, I go, I play* may feature several times. There may be little difference between Satisfactory and Unsatisfactory. **Either or both of the unpredictable bullet points may not have been addressed.** There may be one sentence which is not intelligible to a sympathetic native speaker.	Ability to form tenses is inconsistent. There are errors in many other parts of speech — gender of nouns, cases, singular/plural confusion, for instance. Several errors are serious, perhaps showing mother tongue interference. The detail in the unpredictable bullet points may be very weak. Overall, there is more incorrect than correct.	The candidate copes mainly only with the personal language required in bullet points 1 and 2. The verbs "is" and "study" may also be used correctly. Sentences are basic. An English word may appear in the writing. There may be an example of serious dictionary misuse.

Category	Mark	Content	Accuracy	Language resource — variety, range, structures
Poor	4	The candidate has had considerable difficulty in addressing the job advert. There is little evidence of the use of detailed language. Three or four sentences may not be understood by a sympathetic native speaker. **Either or both of the unpredictable bullet points may not have been addressed.**	Many of the verbs are incorrect. There are many errors in other parts of speech — personal pronouns, gender of nouns, cases, singular/plural confusion, prepositions, for instance. The language is probably inaccurate throughout the writing.	The candidate cannot cope with more than one or two basic verbs. The candidate displays almost no knowledge of the present tense of verbs. Verbs used more than once may be written differently on each occasion. Sentences are very short. The candidate has a very limited vocabulary. Several English words may appear in the writing. There are examples of serious dictionary misuse.
Very poor	0	The candidate is unable to address the job advert. **The two unpredictable bullet points may not have been addressed.** Very little is intelligible to a sympathetic native speaker.	Virtually nothing is correct.	The candidate may only cope with the verbs to have and to be. Very few words are written correctly in the modern language. English words are used. There may be several examples of mother tongue interference. There may be several examples of serious dictionary misuse.

Listening

Item 1

(a) *Any two from:*
- Good/nice atmosphere/ambiance.
- Regular customer(s)/client(s).
  or
  customer(s)/client(s) come(s) back (all the time)
- Never/not boring.

(b) *Any one from:*
- Lives (in a village/town) (quite) far away/doesn't live close/near.
- No/not a lot of (public/other) transport/any specific public transport.

(c) (i) Serving **drink(s)/refreshment(s)/taking drinks orders.**
   (ii) *Any one from:*
   - **Help/aid/assist/work in the kitchen.**
   - Clear/clean/tidy (away) tables.

(d) *Any two from:*
- The customers are **generous**.
- Customers leave (good) tips/she gets (good) tips.
- (she) can eat (for free/at work/at the restaurant/there)/she gets food/to eat/she is allowed her meals (accept any specific meal).

(e) She loves it, but it is busy and tiring.
   (Third box ticked.)
   (NB – More than one box ticked = 0 marks.)

Item 2

(a) Twice/two/2 (evenings/nights/times/days/shifts).

(b) *Any two from:*
- Same/similar age.
- (She has/they have) (a lot of) things in common/similar/same interest(s)/she likes/they like the same thing(s).
- (she likes to/can) **go out** with them/(they like to/can) **go out** together.

(c) (i) **Her friend(s)** met up/used to hang out (at the café)/went (to the café) **without** her/she used to go to a café **with her friend(s).**
   or
   She didn't have (enough) time **for** (her) friend(s)/couldn't/found it difficult to go out with/hang out with/see/meet/hardly saw her **friend(s).**

   (ii) • They meet/she goes/hangs out (with them/friends)/ sees them/friends (on/every) **Friday** (evening).
   • They have a party/go partying/go to parties/have a good time/enjoy themselves.

(d) *Any two from:*
- Organises herself/is (more) organised/organises her time.
- (does it/homework) on a **Sunday**.
- Doesn't spend hours/ages/all her/all the time in front of the television.
  or
  Spends less/not as much time in front of the TV (like/as before).

(e) *Any two from:*
- Has learnt to manage her time.
- (more) confident (speaking/working) **with people** (she doesn't know)/**the public**.
- Become **more** responsible/take on **more** responsibility.

(f) *Any two from:*
- Not sure/doesn't know (yet).
- Look for/find a (full-time/another/a new) job.
- (spend a year) **travelling** in/around/to/through **Europe**.

NATIONAL 5 FRENCH 2015

Reading

Text 1

(a) • (Her) clothes (any spelling)/garments
  • a trip/a holiday/journey/travelling
  (NB – Clothes and holiday interchangeable)

(b) • Asked her **mum's friend/a friend of her mum** (who has a shop)
  • Called/phoned/asked/spoke to the (boss) of a (big) company

(c) To wait/come back/return in two/three years. (Both numbers do not need to be mentioned)/Come back in a couple of years/when she is 17/18.

(d) *Any two from:*
  • During the school holidays
  • (Only if) the school holiday lasts two weeks/15 days/14 days (or more).
  • **Cannot/can't/not allowed to** work **more than** five hours **a day/daily/in the daytime OR can only** work five hours **a day/daily/in the daytime** etc.

(e) • Do/help with housework/cleaning/household chores/chores for an **old(er)/elderly** person
  • Give (individual/particular/private) lessons/courses /tutoring to (younger) pupil(s)/student(s)/children/ help younger people with school work/tutor/teach younger people
  • **Mow/cut** the lawn/garden/grass

Text 2

(a) The Internet is an essential tool at work
  (Second box ticked)
  (NB – More than one box ticked = 0 marks)

(b) *Any two from:*
  • Do/helps with research/investigations
  • communicate with people/students **from around/ all over/across the world/abroad/everywhere/ anywhere**
  • learn computer skills/learn computing

(c) *Any one from:*
  • The child/the student/the pupil can find help/ information/do it (himself/on his own/instead of asking parents) OR they/he/she can find information/help **themselves/himself/on their own**
  • The parent/they can get/give/find **information for/ to inform the child**

(d) (i) *Any one from:*
    • You can lose (any recognisable spelling) contact/touch with reality/real world
    • You read less/fewer books

  (ii) (Stay at home) to chat/discuss/talk/speak with virtual friends/virtually/on the computer/ internet/online.

  (iii) Do not **believe** everything (you read/see/ someone says/writes) (on the internet) **OR** Not everything (you read) (on the internet) **is true/ correct.**

(e) *Any two from:*
  • There are not **enough computer(s)** (in each classroom/room/class).

• The computer/system/network/data system/IT (often) does not work/breaks down
• Difficult/hard to **access/reach/get on to/find** (interesting/web/some) sites/some sites are not **accessible.**

(f) The Internet can support learning when and where appropriate
  (Third box ticked)
  (NB – More than one box ticked = 0 marks)

Text 3

(a) **Perfect** apples

(b) (i) (They have to make/pick/choose) a strict selection (process)/select strictly/strictly select

  (ii) Fruit (and) vegetables/produce with (the slightest) **things wrong/problems/defects/flaws/ with a bit of damage/which are off/not perfect/ which aren't up to standard/scratch/good enough** go in the bin/get thrown away/wasted.

(c) • Buy more than they eat/need/consume/buy too much food/produce/products
  • (In France) **20%** of food is thrown away/wasted/put in the bin
    (NB – We buy more than we eat by 20% = 2 marks)

(d) *Any two from:*
  • Money used in/on food/fruit and veg **production** is wasted/Money we use **to produce** food/fruit and veg is wasted
  • Waste/scrap has to be treated/dealt with/processed /necessary to treat/process waste/recycled
  • Recycling uses/requires/needs/demands (a lot of) energy

(e) • (Make/have/use/write) a shopping list/a list of shopping
  • (Only) buy/get/purchase the right quantity/ amount/produce/food/stuff needed/necessary/ required. **OR** Don't buy unnecessary/too many products/ more than you need.
  • (You can) freeze **leftovers/scraps/food that's left/ the rest/what you don't eat** (in the fridge)

Writing

Please see the assessment criteria for Writing on pages 100–102.

Listening

Item 1

(a) 7 years ago/2008

(b) *Any one from:*
  • To see/watch **20** films/up to **20** films
  • To see film(s) of your choice/to see film(s) you like/ prefer

(c) *Any one from:*
  • (Get to know/appreciate/see/learn about/explore/ understand/experience) different culture(s)/ (it shows/introduces) different culture(s)/ other countries' culture(s)/new culture(s)/(see) differences in other culture(s)
  • Improve your (understanding of) (foreign) language(s)/understand language(s)/learn different/ new language(s)/familiarise yourself with other language(s)/great for learning language(s)

(d) *Any two from:*
- Give your opinion about/view on the film/talk about how good the film was
- Meet/interview/question/speak/talk to (the) actor(s)
- Make/meet (new) friend(s)

(e) *Any one from:*
- A (French) woman/man/person/someone who starts a (new) career/job (in Spain)/finding a (new) career/job (in Spain)
- A (French) woman/man/person/someone who goes to/moves to/is **in Spain**/ lives **in Spain**

(f) To promote international films
(Second box ticked)
(NB – More than one box ticked = 0 marks)

Item 2

(a) *Any one from:*
- It is the (beginning of)/she is on/going on holiday(s)/vacation
- It is her birthday

(b) • Watching films on big screen
- Sharing emotions
(Second and third boxes ticked)
(NB – 3 boxes ticked maximum 1 mark; 4 boxes ticked = 0 marks)

(c) *Any one from:*
- He makes her laugh/he's (really/truly) funny
- She likes his accent (from the North of France)/She enjoys his accent/She likes the way he speaks/He has a nice/good accent
- He has an accent from the North (of France)/ is from the North (of France)/was born in the North (of France)/lives in the North (of France)

(d) *Any two from:*
- They are **too/very/quite/really** long
- The **language** used is old-fashioned/out of date/not modern/ancient
- Not a lot of/little/no **action**/not much happens/not good **action**/(very) slow/boring

(e) *Any two from:*
- Change the channel/ programme/movie/film/it/ watch something else (if you don't like it)
- **Pause/Stop** it to go to the **toilet/bathroom**
- It is free/no charge/you don't have to pay

(f) *Any two from:*
- (Lots of/too much) **advertising**/(too many/lots of) **advert(s)/commercial(s)** (every 10 minutes/are long) **adverts** every 2 minutes
- (Too many) **American** soap(s)/series/sitcom(s)/ show(s)/programme(s)/it's all **American**/it's like **American** TV/**American** TV show(s) are stupid
- (A lot of) stupid game show(s)/quiz(zes) **OR** game show(s)/quiz(zes) **in the morning** OR **stupid** programme(s)/thing(s) **in the morning/every morning**

(g) • **Interesting documentaries/documentary** (any recognisable spelling)
- Programmes in **German/from Germany/German** programmes

Reading
Text 1

(a) Thirteen/13 **year**(s)

(b) (i) • Sand castle (building)**competition**(s)/**contest**(s)
- (Fly) kite(s)/kite flying

  (ii) *Any one from:*
- *Relaxing* **in the sun**
- Reading/read (a book)

(c) Those/people who don't want to miss the **sporting events**/people who (want to/enjoy/rather) watch/see **sporting events** (in the summer)
People who enjoy sporting events

(d) • (Lots/many of them) don't have the **chance/ possibility/opportunity** to go/**can't** go to the sea(side)/beach
or
Gives them/they have the **possibility** to/ **opportunity/chance to** go/they **can** go to the beach
- (They can go) **without leaving/don't need to leave** Paris

(e) *Any one from:*
- *(Great/good) meeting place/point/spot for him and his* **friends**/he can hang out with his **friends**
- It is/was free/he (and his friends)/me (and my friends) can go there for free/they don't have to pay/it doesn't cost.

(f) (i) **Not allowed to/not possible to/do not have the right to/can't** swim/bathe/go bathing there

  (ii) *Any one from:*
- Go to a **sea**(side) resort/the **sea**(side)
- Go to an **outdoor** pool/pool **in the fresh/open air**

Text 2

(a) • Spend/pass (more) time **outdoors/outside**
Like to be outdoors
- To feel/it is safe(r)/(more) secure/has a sense of security

(b) She was bored
(Second box ticked)

(c) • That no one knew her/people didn't know her/she knew no one/didn't know anyone
- A **choice/selection** of entertainment/**a lot of/plenty of/various** things to do

(d) *Any one from:*
- The traffic began/started to **annoy/irritate her/get on her nerves**/the traffic **is annoying/irritated her/ annoyed her**
- **She** was (always) rushed/in a rush/hurry (everyday)

(e) • (Two) dogs (love) **running** in the field(s)/ the countryside
- **Forget** the worries/concerns/problems of **every day/daily** life/she doesn't have to worry about **everyday** life/leaves her **daily** worries behind

(f) • (Take advantage of/benefit from) the bustling **city/ town life**/the busyness/the liveliness of the **city/ town**
 • Quiet/peaceful (life) **in the country(side)**/ tranquillity of **the country(side)**

Text 3

(a) • Having/getting **practical/hands on/useful/helpful/ right** experience
 • Earning/gaining/making/(a little/a bit of) money

(b) *Any two from:*
 • (One in two chance of a placement) being a waste of time/it can be a waste of time
 • (In some/ certain companies you have/there are) **too many/much/lots of** responsibilities
 • (In other/some companies) you (only/just) serve/ make coffee

(c) Managing/doing/handling **new** tasks/du**ties**

(d) (i) • **The boss/manager** was (always) in a bad mood
 • He was **scared/frightened /afraid/ found it difficult/struggled** to ask questions (if he had a problem)

 (ii) *Any two from:*
 • He learned lots/an enormous/tremendous amount (of things)/he was taught a lot
 • He attended/went to (important) meetings
 • He was given/they gave him advice (regularly)

(e) It can be a positive experience but it depends on the company
 (Third box ticked)

Writing

Please see the assessment criteria for Writing on pages 100–102.

Listening

Item 1

(a) *Any one from:*
 • (In) spring
 • Every year/(one week) every year/once a year

(b) *Any two from:*
 • Their hobbies/interests/pastimes/things you like/ are interested in
 • Their animals/pets/animals in their house/ household animals/domestic animals
 • If there are things/foods/is anything they **don't** like eating/to eat/**can't** eat

(c) (i) *Any two from:*
 • Go to a theme park/amusement park/fairground
 • Buy/shop for/get **presents/gifts/souvenirs** (for friend(s))
 • Visit/tour of the town/city, walk around the town/city/town tour(s)

 (ii) *Any one from:*
 Chance to
 • Taste/try specialities **of the country/region /area /Scotland**, eat a traditional/special **Scottish** meal, **national** speciality foods
 • Talk/discuss/speak/tell/chat about/share (the events of) the/his/her/their **day**/how the **day** went/what happened during the **day**

(d) *Any one from:*
 • The people/locals/Scottish (people)/Scots
 • Scenery/countryside/landscape/the views

(e) It is a good way to get know a country well
 (First box ticked)

Item 2

(a) • **24 hour** (coach/bus) journey/ride/she was travelling for **24 hours**
 or
 Long coach/bus journey/ride
 • She was (really) busy/(really) occupied/it was busy (in Scotland) (every day)/she did a lot (of activities) (when she was there)

(b) (i) *Any one from:*
 • (The building/school/it was) well-equipped
 • **Big/large sports** ground(s)/pitch(es)/(playing) field(s)/area(s)/space(s)

 (ii) *Any two from:*
 • Finish/school ends/finishes before/at/by 4pm/16.00
 • **Less** homework/**not as much** homework
 • (Can take part/participate in) activities/clubs/ **at the end of the day/after school**/extra-curricular activities

(c) (i) *Any one from:*
 • (Lively/animated) debate/argument/discussion
 • Did survey(s)/questionnaire(s)

 (ii) • Teacher was passionate/enthusiastic/excited (about subject) really likes/loves (the subject)
 • Explained/explains well/explained/explains the lesson(s)/everything/it (well)/teacher was good at explaining

(d) *Any two from:*
 • The lunch/dinner break is (too/very) short/not long (enough)/not as long/shorter
 • **Just/only** (enough) **time** to eat a sandwich
 • Not enough/not a lot of/not much/no choice in the canteen/there aren't many options in the canteen
 • Meals/menu/food/canteen not balanced/ unbalanced/not healthy

(e) • It's smart
 • They feel proud
 (First and third boxes ticked)

Acknowledgements

Permission has been sought from all relevant copyright holders and Hodder Gibson is grateful for the use of the following:

Image © dibrova/Shutterstock.com (2014 Reading page 2);
Image © Christopher Oates/Shutterstock.com (2014 Reading page 4);
Image © Pierre-Jean Durieu/Shutterstock.com (2014 Reading page 6);
Image © CREATISTA/Shutterstock.com (2015 Reading page 2);
Image © Pressmaster/Shutterstock.com (2015 Reading page 4);
Image © SasPartout/Shutterstock.com (2015 Reading page 6);
Image © ever/Shutterstock.com (2016 Reading page 2);
Image © vvoe/Shutterstock.com (2016 Reading page 4);
Image © David Hughes/Shutterstock.com (2016 Reading page 4);
Image © Ioannis Pantzi/Shutterstock.com (2016 Reading page 6).